I'm becoming

my mother

An Anne Taintor Collection

Anne Taintor

MJF BOOKS
NEW YORK

Published by MJF Books
Fine Communications
322 Eighth Avenue
New York, NY 10001

I'm becoming my mother
LC Control Number 2006923168
ISBN-13: 978-1-56731-789-3
ISBN-10: 1-56731-789-8

Designed by Laura Crookston

This edition published by MJF Books in arrangement
with Chronicle Books LLC.

Printed in Singapore.

MJF Books and the MJF colophon are trademarks
of Fine Creative Media, Inc.

TWP   10   9   8   7   6   5   4   3   2

introduction

Domestically speaking, I was a late bloomer and an early retiree.

My mother saw no reason to teach her daughters the niceties of keeping the hearth. She had a better plan: we would marry men who could afford to hire us help. She always said, "It's just as easy to fall in love with a rich man as it is with a poor man." At eighteen I left home knowing how to wash and dry dishes, period.

To this day, I don't resemble anyone's domestic ideal, though I still deeply appreciate the pleasures of a well run home: floor swept and larder stocked. And I truly prefer a home-cooked meal to dinner in a fine restaurant any day. Lucky for me that I ended up with a man who cooks and cleans and shops. He can even find things in the refrigerator. So, domesticity is bliss . . . especially when someone else does it all for you.

Mom nearly had it right.

—**Anne Taintor**

gosh, he went well with her drapes

you're wearing *that?*

cash
is for
amateurs

change

your

shoes...

change your life!

frugal is such an *ugly* word

she had made

yet *another*

wise shopping decision

they put
the "funk"
in functional

am I
the last sane person
on this planet?

relax son,
finding things in the fridge
is
women's work

does one serve *red* or *green* chili with a pinot noir?

her presentation was flawless

can't

make

me...

she always enjoyed receiving gender-specific gifts

okay,

so the family

wasn't

functional,

but at least their gifts were

she liked to

stir things up

we are all
utterly unclean

he kind of enjoyed

taking orders

she had done

a *fabulous* job

with him

escape

I am *devoted* to yardwork

my garden

kicks

ass

I'm happy…

yet I'm aware

of the

ironic ramifications

of my happiness

a career...

a family

to care for...

gee! I've got it all!

I refuse to let common sense cloud my judgment

domestically

disabled

...and the

neighbors

are

darlings!

am I living happily ever after yet?

I'm having a senior moment

because I'm the mother,

that's why

if it's not one thing, it's your mother